# Simply Science

# POWERFUL MACHINES

## Discover Science Through Facts and Fun

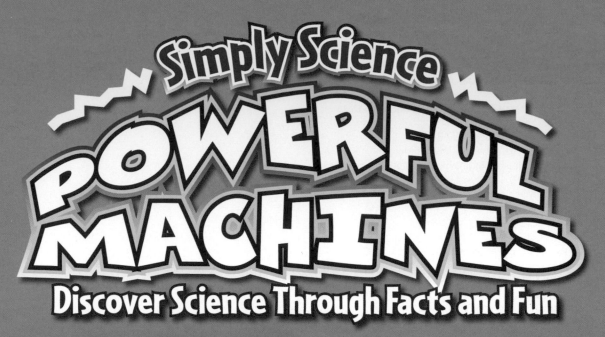

By Gerry Bailey

Science and curriculum consultant:

Debra Voege, M.A., science curriculum resource teacher

Gareth Stevens
Publishing

Please visit our web site at www.garethstevens.com.
For a free catalog describing our list of high-quality books, call 1-800-542-2595 (USA)
or 1-800-387-3178 (Canada). Our fax: 1-877-542-2596

**Library of Congress Cataloging-in-Publication Data**
Bailey, Gerry.
      Powerful machines / By Gerry Bailey.
          p. cm.—(Simply Science)
      Includes bibliographical references and index.
      ISBN-10: 1-4339-0035-1   ISBN-13: 978-1-4339-0035-8 (lib. bdg.)
      1. Machinery—Juvenile literature. I. Title.
  TJ147.B33   2008
  621.8—dc22                      2008027568

This North American edition first published in 2009 by
**Gareth Stevens Publishing**
A Weekly Reader® Company
1 Reader's Digest Road
Pleasantville, NY 10570-7000 USA

This edition copyright © 2009 by Gareth Stevens, Inc. Original edition copyright © 2007 by
Diverta Publishing Ltd., First published in Great Britain by Diverta Publishing Ltd., London, UK.

Gareth Stevens Executive Managing Editor: Lisa M. Herrington
Gareth Stevens Creative Director: Lisa Donovan
Gareth Stevens Designer: Keith Plechaty
Gareth Stevens Associate Editor: Amanda Hudson
Gareth Stevens Publisher: Keith Garton
Special thanks to Jessica Cohn

**Photo Credits:** Cover (tc) Thomas Sztanek/Shutterstock Inc.; (bl) ESA/CNES/ARIANESPACE-Service Optique CSG; p.5 Sharon
Meredith/Shutterstock Inc.; p. 8 Alan Egginton/Shutterstock Inc.; p. 10 Jeff Gynane/Shutterstock Inc.; p. 15 Carolyn M.
Carpenter/Shutterstock Inc.; p. 17 Ponomareva Yevgeniya/Shutterstock Inc.; p. 19 (bl) John Leung/Shutterstock Inc., (tr)
S.H.K./CORBIS SYGMA; p. 20 (l) Uli/Shutterstock Inc.; pp. 20–21 qaphotos.com/Alamy; p. 22 (t) Gary L. Brewer/Shutterstock Inc., (b)
Thomas Sztanek/Shutterstock Inc.; p. 23 (tl) Craig Aurness/CORBIS, (cl) Chris Alan Wilton/Alamy, (r) ESA/CNES/ARIANESPACE-Service
Optique CSG; p. 26 Y. Shira/Rice University; p. 27 (t) Scott Bauer/US Department of Agriculture/Science Photo Library, (br) Eye of
Science/Science Photo Library; p. 29 (tl) Evening Standard/Getty Images, (tr) Oliver Uhrig/Shutterstock Inc.

**Illustrations:** Steve Boulter, Q2a Media

**Diagrams:** Karen Radford

Every effort has been made to trace the copyright holders for the photos used in this book, and
the publisher apologizes in advance for any unintentional omissions. We would be pleased to insert the appropriate
acknowledgements in any subsequent edition of this publication.

Printed in the United States of America

1 2 3 4 5 6 7 8 9 13 12 11 10 09 08

# CONTENTS

# Powerful Machines

What do you think of when you think of a machine? Maybe you think of a machine that helps your family do things around the house, such as a washing machine. Some people might think of something simple, such as a hammer. Even a hammer is a machine. Machines help people do work.

Larger machines often need to be powered by electricity or another kind of energy. Simple machines just need people to move them and make them work.

Machines can be powered by **you** ...

by an **ox** or a **horse** ...

or by the **Sun**.

They can be powered by **electricity** ...

by burning a fuel like **gasoline** ...

by making **steam** ...

or even by **nuclear power**.

Powerful machines like this truck are powered by gasoline.

# Simple Machines

Machines don't have to be big to be useful. Almost all machines are based on some very simple ones. There are six basic "simple machines." They are at work in almost every tool and machine you use.

## Six Simple Machines

The six simple machines are: the **lever**, **wheel and axle**, **pulley**, **wedge**, **ramp**, and **screw**.

lever

wheel and axle

wedge

pulley

ramp

screw

## A Pick Ax

A pick ax is two simple machines in one: a lever and a wedge. The handle is a lever. You power the ax as you would power a hammer. The end piece is a wedge, which can drive apart dirt and stones as it bears down.

## Can Opener

A can opener is made of three simple machines. The handle has levers. They push a sharp wheel rim, or wedge, into a can's top. The person opening the can turns a wheel and axle to cut off the can's top.

**handle**

**sharp rim of wheel**

## A Screwdriver

A screwdriver uses twisting power to ease a screw into material. The screwdriver is really a long screw itself. The screw's thread, or ridge, acts like a long ramp! That eases the screw into the material slowly, one full turn at a time.

## A Claw Hammer

A claw hammer works as a lever to bang nails into wood or other material. The claw pulls out nails. It's the **load end** of the lever. The top of the hammerhead is the **fulcrum**. That's the point at which a lever turns as it moves things.

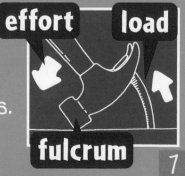

**effort**  **load**

**fulcrum**

# Animal Power

A plow is a tool. It carves a groove, or furrow, into a field. That rut is a place where seeds can be planted.

A plow has a handle. It has a blade that acts as a wedge. The wedge pushes earth apart and then turns it over.

Early plows were probably first used in China and the Middle East. Oxen or horses pulled the first plows. Modern plows have many rows of steel blades. They are pulled by powerful tractors.

**1.** When people began farming, they probably just threw seed onto the ground. Birds probably ate much of the seed. The seed needed to be sown deeper into the ground.

# A Wedge for Plowing

**2.** People probably tried using sticks to make holes for seed. That would have taken a long time, however.

**3.** Farmers used sticks to scrape furrows. It would, however, have been hard to make deep furrows that way.

**4.** An ax is strong enough to hack holes or furrows in hard ground. The wedge of the blade cuts through the earth easily.

**5.** When farmers attached a wedge to a wooden frame, they had a plow, a machine animals could pull.

9

# Push Power

A wheelbarrow is made up of two simple machines—a lever and a wheel and axle.

The axle is actually the fulcrum of the lever. The wheel works to cut down rubbing, or **friction**, as the wheelbarrow moves along the ground.

Simple machines work together to make a task easier for us to do.

A **lever** helps raise loads—the handle of the wheelbarrow is a lever.

A **wheel and axle** helps move loads smoothly along the ground.

**1.** Long ago, if people wanted to move things from place to place, they had to carry it all or balance it on their heads.

**2.** Then people used a wheel-less wagon. It was a box that was dragged on runners. They could carry more in this early wagon, but it was still hard work.

# A Wheel Helps Carry Loads

**3.** When the wheel was invented, things began to change. Large wagons could be pulled by horses. A much smaller kind of wagon, with one wheel, could be pushed by a person. The **load** just had to spread around the wheel the right way.

**4.** People figured out a way to build a board around a wheel and axle, spreading the load the right way. Then they added handles. This machine was the first wheelbarrow.

**5.** A modern wheelbarrow has a V-shaped frame fixed to a wheel and axle. The box, or barrow, fits onto the frame. A pair of handles are attached for people to hold.

# The Cotton Gin

Cotton is a plant with fluff and seeds inside its seedpods, or bolls. Cotton fiber is harvested and used to make fabric.

The pickers used to remove the seeds from the bolls as they picked. This was a lot of trouble!

*It's cotton picking time again!*

## A Machine to Clean Cotton

**1.** By the late 1700s, cotton was a popular fabric for clothing in America. Eli Whitney lived in the South, where much of the cotton was being grown.

**2.** There was a problem. It took pickers a whole day to separate out the seeds as they gathered the cotton.

## How the Gin Worked

The cotton gin fixed the problem. The cotton bolls were put into the top of the machine. As the handle turned, cotton was fed through wire teeth. That combed out seeds. A brush roller removed the cotton from the wire teeth.

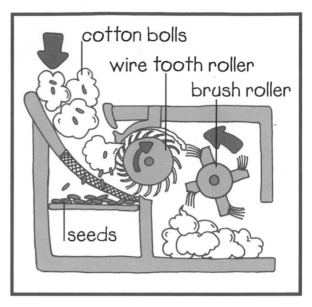

cotton bolls

wire tooth roller

brush roller

seeds

**3.** Whitney knew it would be far quicker to remove the seeds by machine—some kind of mechanical brush. Nothing like that had been invented yet.

**4.** He came up with the idea of a brush-and-roller machine. He made a **cylinder** with wire teeth to pull the fibers through tiny holes. Then he added a roller with brushes to remove the fiber from the teeth. The rollers were wound with a handle. His cotton gin was a huge success.

# Nature's Machine

The sundial is one of our early tools. It tells the time of day.

A sundial has a marked plate. A pointer is fixed to the middle. That pointer or pin is called a gnomon. The pointer casts a shadow when in sunlight.

Time to stop working!

## A Shadow Tells Time

**1.** Long ago, people used the Sun to guess what time of day it was.

**2.** The Sun was high in the middle of the day, and it was low at the start and finish.

**3.** People noticed that the Sun cast shadows as it moved position during the course of the day. They tried to find a way to measure the shadows.

## Casting a Shadow

Around the edges is a time **scale** marked in hours. When the Sun shines, it makes the pointer, or gnomon, cast a shadow onto the scale. As the angle of the Sun changes in the sky, the shadow moves, showing the hour.

**4.** The people wanted to record times to feed the animals or do work around  the house. They wanted to be able to say exactly how long a journey took.

**5.** This led to the invention of the sundial. A round plate was marked with the hours. A pointer in the middle cast a shadow. You could read the hour on which the shadow fell.

# Spring Power

**1.** Ever since clocks were invented, we have been able to tell time. We can read seconds, minutes, and hours.

**2.** As long as you can see a clock, you know what time it is. You know if you're too late or too early.

**3.** Early clocks used weights called pendulums. The weight would swing. The movement would move the hands of the clock.

**4.** These clocks were heavy. They were large. Carrying a big, heavy clock would not be easy at all! People needed something else.

**5.** It became clear that a smaller clock powered by something lighter than a pendulum would be quite helpful.

**6.** A coiled spring, which can be small, has energy stored in it. Clockmakers found that springs could power tiny clocks worn on chains or on wrists. These small clocks were called watches.

# Time Tools

A wristwatch is a tool for telling time. It is worn on the wrist. It can use a small coiled spring for its power.

A spring is a coiled piece of flat wire. If you push the spring out of shape, it goes back to how it was. It springs back. A spring that is pushed out of shape has energy which is ready to use. The **stored energy** is turned into movement when the spring is released. The first watches used this kind of energy for power.

Many clocks and other gadgets use coiled springs to move the parts inside. ▶

# Engines for Machines

Large machines need more than muscle power or springs to keep them working. They need a much stronger source of power. They need engines! Here are engines that have changed our world.

## Gas Engine

An internal combustion engine makes an explosion inside. A mix of air and gas causes the explosion. In a car, the explosion pushes down pistons. The pistons turn a crank. The crank is connected by a shaft to the wheels outside.

## Steam Engine

The first **steam engines** were large and not very efficient. Richard Trevithick's high-pressure steam engine changed all that. It was small enough and powerful enough to be used in mines. It helped us develop the steam locomotive and the railway system.

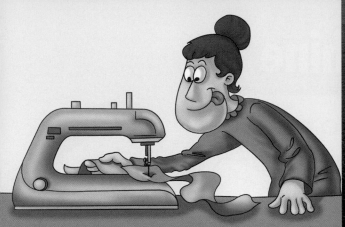

## Electric Engine

Michael Faraday invented a **dynamo**, an electricity-making machine. That made it possible to invent an electric motor. Electricity and **magnetism** make a rod turn, which runs a piece of machinery, such as a sewing machine or a train.

## Atomic Engine

When the nucleus, or middle part, of an atom is split, it makes a huge amount of energy in a blast. This blast can be used to power engines—if you're careful! Atomic, or nuclear, submarines use atomic power to turn their propellers. These vehicles can run for a decade without refueling.

Fast electric trains can move at speeds over 348 miles (560 kilometers) per hour!

# A Giant of a Machine

Sometimes, if you want to do a big job, you need a big piece of machinery to do it. Huge machines, like rock drills, can help with some pretty tough work.

This huge machine is an earthmover, or excavator. It moves heavy soil and rock from one place to another.

This machine helps build underground tunnels.

# Land, Sea, and Air Movers

Machines make up many forms of transportation. These machines get faster as new kinds of energy and technical gadets are discovered to power them.

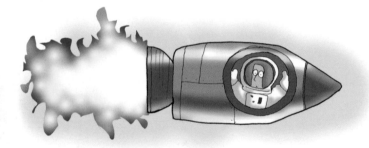

This train, carrying iron from Mauritania to Morocco, is probably the world's longest train. It can stretch to as long as 2 miles (3 kilometers)!

The Terex Titan is the world's largest **dump truck**. It can carry huge loads up to 386 tons.

**Supertankers** weigh thousands of tons. These are the world's largest ships. They are able to transport two or three million barrels of oil across the seas.

The world's biggest plane is the Russian-built **Antonov 225**. It is used to carry air cargo. This huge airplane can carry 80 cars across land and sea!

The **Ariane rocket** needs a huge amount of power to be thrust into space.

# Electric Machines

Most of the machines we see are powered by electricity.

Electricity is often created by a generator, which has a series of wire coils spinning between two magnets. The coils are spun by a **turbine** that can be driven by wind, water, or steam. The electricity generated is distributed to your home by a network of metal cables.

Electricity can also come from a battery, which turns chemical energy into electrical energy.

## Cell Phone

A cell phone, or mobile phone, is actually a small radio, or walkie-talkie. It is an electrical machine that sends messages along sound frequencies. The frequencies are picked up and passed on from one transmitter to another. Transmitters work in a particular geographical area known as a cell. The cells are linked so messages can pass from cell to cell as you move and talk.

## Pacemaker

A pacemaker can help a heart function properly. It's a machine powered by a small battery. It sends electrical impulses to the heart to help it beat more regularly.

## ATV

An Advanced Tethered Vehicle, also called an ATV, is an electric-powered submersible. It runs without someone on it. It can be used for exploring wrecks on the ocean floor.

## Computer

Computers use electrical pulses that go on and off. The first computers used large vacuum tubes to make the pulses go on and off, so they were huge—the size of rooms! In 1947, small on-off switches called transistors were invented. That allowed computers to be smaller and faster. Then microchips appeared. They had several tiny transistors clustered together on each microchip. There were about ten transistors on each microchip at first—now there can be a billion!

# Working With Atoms

Imagine a machine so small you can't actually see it. In fact, it's so small you could get 20,000 of them onto a human hair. This incredible machine is a nanomachine. It's created through something known as **nanotechnology**.

Nano (or tiny) technology means working with things measured in nanometers. A nanometer is one billionth of a meter—and that's very, very small!

Everything we see, from trees to moths, was built one atom at a time. So scientists believe they should be able to invent things by building them one atom at a time as well. That's nanotechnology. An atom, in case you were wondering, is 10 nanometers wide.

## Nanocar

The funny-looking machine below is actually a tiny car: a nanocar. It was built from just a few atoms, which are small particles within elements. The car has a rotating motor powered by light. It has a frame and four axles. The wheels are molecules!

## Electron Microscopes

Electron microscopes use beams of electrons. Electrons are the tiny parts of an atom that spin around a nucleus. These beams let us see better than regular microscopes do. We can see inside cells. We can even see chemicals like DNA!

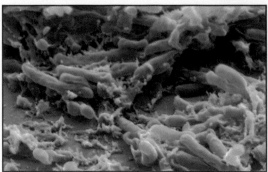

Tiny bacteria can be seen using an electron microscope.

# The Robot

A robot is a machine that can do jobs without help from humans. Some robots carry out jobs that repeat. Others do dangerous jobs, such as working inside nuclear reactors or with harmful liquids.

> The word *robot* comes from the Czech word *robata,* meaning "hard work."

## A Machine for Routine Jobs

**1.** In large factories, hundreds of workers are needed to do different jobs. Some of these jobs take up a great deal of the workers' time.

**2.** The factories wanted to make the work go faster. They also wanted to find a way of cutting costs. Hiring workers to do easy, routine jobs is expensive.

## The First Robot

At first, scientists tried to develop robots that looked like people. In 1932, a robot called Alpha was shown in London. It could read, bow, tell the time, sing, and smoke cigars!

Alpha

Large mechanical robots perform simple tasks in a car factory.

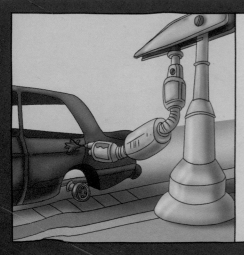

**3.** Inventors came up with machines that could do repetitive jobs, such as welding panels on cars. These machines are robots.

**4.** Robots follow a series of instructions programmed into them. Usually a robot contains a computer called the control system. This computer acts like an electronic brain. The computer program makes the robot repeat and check its tasks.

# Powerful Machines Quiz

1. How many simple machines make up a can opener?

2. Name an electric machine that moves heavy soil.

3. How long is a nanometer?

4. What type of machine gets seeds out of cotton fibers?

5. Name an electric machine that helps keep a heart beating.

6. Who invented the high-pressure steam engine?

7. What happens if a spring is pushed out of shape?

8. Name simple machines in a wheelbarrow.

9. Why won't a sundial gnomon work in the dark?

10. When does an ox pull a wedge?

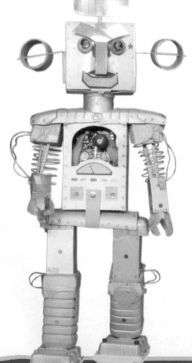

# Glossary

**cylinder:** a solid figure that has two circular bases and a main surface at right angles, or perpendicular, to both of those bases

**dynamo:** a generator that produces a direct current, or flow of electricity

**friction:** the rubbing of two objects, which can slow their movement

**fulcrum:** the point of support on a lever, a bar that raises or lowers things

**lever:** a simple machine that is a bar turning around a fixed point of support

**load:** the measure of weight, which can vary by how a thing is held or moved

**load end:** the end of a lever that conveys the load, or weight, of something

**magnetism:** the force of attraction associated with electricity on the move

**nanotechnology:** the creation of equipment made of atoms and molecules

**pulley:** a simple machine that is a wheel used to raise weight

**ramp:** a simple machine that is a slope used for moving weight between levels

**scale:** a series of marks at regular spaces, used in measurement

**screw:** a simple machine that is a cylinder with a ramp wrapped around it

**steam engines:** machines that use steam to move a mechanism

**stored energy:** the energy, caused by a thing's position, waiting for release

**turbine:** a device spun by a flow of energy working on a system of fans

**wedge:** a simple machine that can be driven into a thing to split or break it

**wheel and axle:** a simple machine with a turning pin on which a wheel turns

# Index

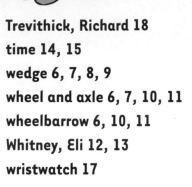